I0539502

A FRAMEWORK FOR HOW TO DO AN IN-DEPTH STUDY OF SCRIPTURE USING THE LIFE OF JOHN THE BAPTIST

Published 2025

ISBN: 979-8-218-49738-5

A FRAMEWORK FOR HOW TO DO AN IN-DEPTH STUDY OF SCRIPTURE USING THE LIFE OF JOHN THE BAPTIST

Scripture quotations in this book are taken from the following translations:

King James Version (KJV) – Public Domain

1599 Geneva Bible (GNV) – Public Domain

New Living Translation (NLT) Scripture quotations taken from the Holy Bible, New Living Translation. Copyright © 1996, 2004, 2015 by Tyndale House Foundation. Used by permission of Tyndale House Publishers, Inc., Carol Stream, Illinois 60188. All rights reserved.

New International Version (NIV) Scripture quotations taken from the Holy Bible, New International Version®, NIV®. Copyright © 1973, 1978, 1984, 2011 by Biblica, Inc.™ Used by permission. All rights reserved worldwide.

New American Standard Bible (NASB) Scripture quotations taken from the New American Standard Bible®. Copyright © 1960, 1962, 1963, 1968, 1971, 1972, 1973, 1975, 1977, 1995, 2020 by The Lockman Foundation. Used by permission. All rights reserved.

Amplified® Bible (AMP) Scripture quotations taken from the Amplified® Bible. Copyright © 2015 by The Lockman Foundation. Used by permission. All rights reserved.

Names of God Bible (NOG) Scripture quotations taken from the Names of God Bible™. Copyright © 2011 by Baker Publishing Group. Used by permission. All rights reserved.

New Catholic Bible (NCB) Scripture quotations taken from the New Catholic Bible®. Copyright © 2019 by Catholic Book Publishing Corp. Used by permission. All rights reserved.

God's Word® Translation (GW) Scripture quotations taken from GOD'S WORD® Translation. Copyright © 1995 by God's Word to the Nations. Used by permission. All rights reserved.

Hebrew names, transliterations, and renderings of God and Jesus referenced in this workbook are derived from the following sources:

GOD'S WORD® Translation. Copyright © 1995 by God's Word to the Nations

CEPHER: Copyright © by Cepher Publishing Group, LLC

These sources are cited for linguistic and educational reference purposes only.

The New World Translation of the Holy Scriptures (NWT) is cited in limited instances for the purpose of textual comparison only. Its inclusion is not an endorsement of Jehovah's Witness theology and is used solely to highlight differences in translation choices when compared with widely accepted Bible versions.

Scripture quotations taken from the New World Translation (NWT). Copyright © 1961, 1970, 1971, 1984, 2013 by Watch Tower Bible and Tract Society of Pennsylvania. Used for comparative and educational purposes.

A FRAMEWORK FOR HOW TO DO AN IN-DEPTH STUDY OF SCRIPTURE USING THE LIFE OF JOHN THE BAPTIST

TABLE OF CONTENTS

ABOUT THE STUDY

The purpose of this study is to give you an in-depth look and framework on how you can study The Word of God. There are many ways to approach studying the Bible. The most important approach is to first pray and ask The Holy Spirit to guide and direct you in understanding and wisdom.

Before starting with John's life, there is a lesson on the versions of the Bible to encourage you to compare Bible translations. A bonus lesson about the Names of God gives an opportunity for you to consider the power in His many names and attributes.

As we look at the Life of John the Baptist, it starts with his birth announcement and concludes with his death. In this study we discover what John thought about himself, what Jesus said about him, and what the disciples and others believed about John the Baptist.

Below are some points to keep in mind as you go through this study:

- Various translations are used, such as the King James Version (KJV), the New Living Translation (NLT), the New International Version (NIV), the New American Standard Bible (NASB), the Names of God Bible (NOG), the Amplified Bible (AMP), and the New Catholic Bible (NCB).
- Some sections may not direct you to read certain verses, but I encourage you to read all Bible verses listed.
- Each Lesson includes questions and reflections to encourage you to meditate on what you are learning and to go further in your study.
- Not all Lessons are the same in length; give yourself whatever time you choose before going to the next lesson.

While there are various versions and interpretations of Scripture, the foundational message of The Father, The Son, and The Spirit is consistent with all versions used. This consistency confirms that salvation only comes through our Savior, The One who died on the cross and rose again.

I hope this journey will help you deepen your knowledge of our Creator, how to live for Him, and provide insight into a framework for how to do an in-depth study of the Bible. Studying Scripture and growing in your relationship with The Lord, is a life-long and rewarding journey.

LESSON 1

WHY & HOW TO STUDY THE BIBLE

The richness of the Bible and the ways of our Creator are beyond what we can comprehend and imagine. Bible study is critical if you are to learn and grow in your faith. There is never a time when we have done enough studying. You may have read a verse many times; and yet, each time you approach Scripture, something new can be revealed to you. Let's explore why Bible study is important.

<u>2 Timothy 3:16-17</u> (NLT)
16 All Scripture is inspired by God and is useful to teach us what is true and to make us realize what is wrong in our lives. 17 It corrects us when we are wrong and teaches us to do what is right. God uses it to prepare and equip his people to do every good work.

<u>Psalm 119:11</u> (KJV)
Thy word have I hid in mine heart, that I might not sin against thee.

<u>2 Timothy 2:15</u> (KJV)
Study to shew thyself approved unto God, a workman that needeth not to be ashamed, rightly dividing the word of truth.

Let's look at what Timothy says "rightly dividing the word of truth." This means to be careful and skillful in teaching the truth.

Questions for Discussion:

1. Why do you think it's important to study the Bible?

2. What is the difference between reading the Bible and studying the Bible?

3. Who or what forces would want to keep you from studying Scripture and seeking truth? Why?

Whether you read or study the Bible, first start by praying. Ask The Holy Spirit to give you wisdom and understanding, and trust that He will guide you into truth.

As you begin your study, it is helpful to have an overview before you start. For example, if you want to study the book of Romans, first read the entire book for a general understanding. If you are reading about someone, such as Moses, you may decide to take it step by step starting from whatever information you can learn from the earliest part of his life to where and how his story ends. It may be helpful to understand what was happening before and during Moses' time as well as the leaders or groups of people involved, and the customs and culture of that time period.

There are times that you may not have much information about your topic or person of interest. For example, little is known about the prophet Elijah. The Bible does tell us that he was a Tishbite, who was from Gilead. In 1 Chronicles 8:27 the name Elijah is mentioned as a descendant of Benjamin. This might be the same Elijah the Tishbite, however, it is uncertain. Finally, it is helpful to know something about the author of the book you are studying in Scripture.

It's beneficial to actively engage with the text. For example, you can highlight verses and write notes directly in the Bible, take notes on paper, or use a computer. This practice will allow you to retain information and serves as a valuable resource for revisiting specific points or participating in discussions with others.

Reflection:

Someone once told me a story they had heard about Eve, the mother of our human race. It was so far-fetched and nothing that I had seen in any Bible verse throughout Scripture. As they were talking to me, I couldn't help but imagine them repeating this story to others who may have simply accepted their word as truth. When someone tells you what the Bible says, verify the information by doing your own research and asking them to tell you where in the Bible is their point of reference. Praying and seeking guidance from The Holy Spirit helps you to discern what is true. Note what Jesus says about truth in the verses below:

John 8:32 (NASB)
And you will know the truth, and the truth will set you free.

John 8:44 (NIV)
You belong to your father, the devil, and you want to carry out your father's desires. He was a murderer from the beginning, not holding to the truth, for there is no truth in him. When he lies, he speaks his native language, for he is a liar and the father of lies.

<u>John 16:13</u> (AMP)
But when He, The Spirit of Truth, comes, He will guide you into all the truth [full and complete truth]. For He will not speak on His own initiative, but He will speak whatever He hears [from The Father—the message regarding The Son], and He will disclose to you what is to come [in the future].

Before I start to read or study the Bible, I pray and ask The Holy Spirit to open my mind and heart to see what He wants me to know and apply to my life. We need to remember that The Scriptures have been given to us and preserved by The Supernatural Power of The Almighty God. And, it is this power that will guide us into truth, if that is the desire of our hearts.

Questions for Further Study:

- Who told us to study Scripture and why?
- What happens when you don't study?
- How does the Bible help us in our everyday lives?
- Who or what would you like to study?
- What insights have you learned from this lesson?

Your Reflections:

Additional responses to questions and/or notes:

LESSON 2

PRAYER, PRAISE, & WORSHIP

In this Lesson, we discuss the importance of prayer, praise, and worship. I encourage you to start your day with prayer and thankfulness. God wants to have a relationship with us and His invitation is daily—as evidenced by the miracle and gift of waking up each day.

The Bible is filled with verses about prayer. It talks about why we should pray, how to pray, how others prayed, and how prayer transforms our lives. When we pray, we are inviting God to speak to our hearts through the power of The Holy Spirit; we are in essence inviting Him to have a relationship with us.

> Colossians 4:2 (NIV)
> *Devote yourselves to prayer, being watchful and thankful.*

> Jeremiah 29:12 (NIV)
> *Then you will call on me and come and pray to me, and I will listen to you.*

> Romans 12:12 (NIV)
> *Be joyful in hope, patient in affliction, faithful in prayer.*

Praise and Worship is a way that God connects with us and we with Him. It allows for a time of reflection and thankfulness on who He is, what He has done, and what He will do. Praising God is thanking Him through word or song.

When you worship God, you are demonstrating a strong feeling of respect, love, and admiration. When you praise God, you are also worshiping Him.

Read the following verses:
Psalm 66:4
Psalm 100
Psalm 150:1-6
Ezra 3:10-11
2 Samuel 6:14-15

Questions for Discussion:

1. How should you approach reading and studying God's Word?

2. How has praying helped you?

3. Do you engage in praise and worship? If so, how has it helped you?

4. What are other things or beings that people worship, and why is it harmful to worship them?

5. Why is it important to pray, praise, and worship God?

Prayer, Praise, and Worship is an example of your love for God, which Jesus says is the greatest commandment.

> Mark 12:30 (NIV)
> *Love the Lord your God with all your heart and with all your soul and with all your mind and with all your strength.*

Reflection:

Starting with prayer and incorporating praise and worship helps us get ready to study the Bible in a meaningful way that allows us to be open to hearing from God. I start my day with prayer and then typically with a devotional or a study of someone or a topic in Scripture. I listen to my favorite worship music before listening to anything else. I believe this practice helps me start my day with the intention of putting God first in my life—even if I don't always succeed.

Questions for Further Study:

What are other verses about prayer, praise, and worship?
Why do you think prayer, praise, and worship is important to God?
What insights have you learned from this lesson?

Your Reflections:

Additional responses to questions and/or notes:

LESSON 3

VERSIONS OF THE BIBLE

This lesson looks at the various translations of the Bible. It touches on how removing even one word can have a profound impact. In the ancient days, people received messages directly from God, or from the prophets, priests, and other leaders. The sacred and inspired writings of Scripture have been preserved for thousands of years.

2 Timothy 3:16-17 (King James Version—KJV)
All scripture is given by inspiration of God, and is profitable for doctrine, for reproof, for correction, for instruction in righteousness. [17] That the man of God may be perfect, thoroughly furnished unto all good works.

2 Timothy 3:16-17 (New Living Translation—NLT)
All Scripture is inspired by God and is useful to teach us what is true and to make us realize what is wrong in our lives. It corrects us when we are wrong and teaches us to do what is right. [17] God uses it to prepare and equip his people to do every good work.

Today the Bible is readily available, and with the advancement of technology; it has been mass produced and translated in numerous languages. These translations are consistent with the foundational message of The Gospel—All things were created by God, The Creator dwelt among us in the flesh, and The Spirit of God is guiding and directing our lives.

Read the following verses and compare it with several translations of the Bible:

Genesis 1:1-3
John 1:1-3
Isaiah 9:6
Matthew 2:1-6
Luke 2:8-12
John 1:41
John 14:6
John 14:16-17
John 14:26

8

The following is a sample list of English Bible translations:
- The Geneva Bible (GNV). Printed in 1560
- King James Version (KJV). Translated in 1611, and considered the most accurate Bible translation in the world.
- New Catholic Bible (NCB). Published 2002-2015
- New American Standard Bible (NASB). The book of John was completed in 1960 and the completed Bible in 1971.
- New International Version (NIV). Translated in 1978
- New Living Translation (NLT). Translated in 1996

Let's compare Bible translations:

Genesis 1:1-2

(Geneva Bible—GNV)
1 In the beginning God created the heauen and the earth. 2 And the earth was without forme and void, and darkenesse was vpon the deepe, and the Spirit of God mooued vpon the waters.

(King James Version—KJV)
1 In the beginning God created the heaven and the earth. 2 And the earth was without form, and void; and darkness was upon the face of the deep. And the Spirit of God moved upon the face of the waters.

John 3:1-2

(New Living Translation—NLT)
1 There was a man named Nicodemus, a Jewish religious leader who was a Pharisee. 2 After dark one evening, he came to speak with Jesus. "Rabbi," he said, "we all know that God has sent you to teach us. Your miraculous signs are evidence that God is with you."

(Geneva Bible—GNV)
1 There was nowe a man of the Pharises, named Nicodemus, a ruler of the Iewes. 2 This man came to Iesus by night, and sayd vnto him, Rabbi, we knowe ye thou art a teacher come from God: for no man could doe these miracles that thou doest, except God were with him.

Genesis 10:5

(King James Version—KJV)
By these were the isles of the Gentiles divided in their lands; every one after his tongue, after their families, in their nations.

Genesis 10:5

(New American Standard Bible—NASB)
From these the people of the coastlands of the nations were separated into their lands, every one according to his language, according to their families, into their nations.

Genesis 10:20

(King James Version—KJV)
These are the sons of Ham, after their families, after their tongues, in their countries, and in their nations.

(New American Standard Bible—NASB)
These are the sons of Ham, according to their families, according to their languages, by their lands, and by their nations.

Genesis 10:31

(King James Version—KJV)
These are the sons of Shem, after their families, after their tongues, in their lands, after their nations.

(New American Standard Bible—NASB)
These are the sons of Shem, according to their families, according to their languages, by their lands, and according to their nations.

In addition to the translation(s) you currently use, I suggest that you incorporate the King James Version, which as previously stated is considered the most accurate Bible translation in the world. A misinterpreted word can change the meaning of a verse entirely. For example see two translations below from Ezekiel 39:28.

King James Version (KJV)
Then they shall know that I am the Lord their God, which caused them to be led into captivity among the heathen: but I have gathered them unto their own land, and have left none of them any more there.

New American Standard Bible (NASB)
Then they will know that I am the LORD their God because I made them go into exile among the nations, and then gathered them again to their own land; and I will leave none of them there any longer.

The KJV says that the Israelites were led into captivity. When you are in captivity, you are being taken by force—it is not voluntary. However, the NASB uses the word "exile," which can carry an entirely different meaning. *Exile* can refer either to being forcibly removed from one's country or home, or to a voluntary absence.

Questions for Discussion:

1. What do you notice about the Geneva Bible (GNV) compared to the other versions?

2. What do you notice about the translations in Genesis that talk about the sons of Noah?

3. Why do you think it may be helpful to compare versions of the Bible?

In addition to translations there are also transliterations.

Vocabulary.com
> "*Transliteration* is the process of transferring a word from the alphabet of one language to another. *Transliteration* helps people pronounce words and names in foreign languages."

> "*Unlike a translation, which tells you the meaning of a word that's written in another language, a transliteration only gives you an idea of how the word is pronounced, by putting it in a familiar alphabet. It changes the letters from the word's original alphabet to similar-sounding letters in a different one. In Hebrew, the Jewish winter holiday is חנוכה. Its English transliteration is Hanukkah or Chanukah.*"

Finally, let's briefly discuss the Jehovah's Witness Bible, called "The New World Translation (NWT)." It was first released in 1950, which is almost 400 years after the Geneva Bible and over 300 years after the King James Version. The Jehovah Witness Bible is not considered to be a translation or transliteration, but a different belief from the widely recognized three major historic divisions of Christianity—all of which are consistent with the King James Version as it relates to who Jesus is:

1. Catholic (i.e., Roman Catholic Church)
2. Orthodox (e.g., Ethiopian Orthodox, Coptic Orthodox, Greek Orthodox, and Russian Orthodox)
3. Protestant (e.g., Baptist, Methodist, Presbyterian, Lutheran, non-denominational)

We will compare a few verses from the Jehovah Witness Bible (NWT) with the King James Version (KJV) to understand how it is significantly different from other Bible translations.

John 1:1 (King James Version—KJV)
"In the beginning was the Word, and the Word was with God, and the Word was God."

John 1:1 (Jehovah Witness Bible—NWT)
"In the beginning was the Word, and the Word with God, and the Word was a god."

The KJV says that "The Word was God." This means that The Word (Jesus) was God—equal to God. The meaning conveys that Jesus is Divine. The Jehovah Witness Bible inserts the letter "a" and replaces the capital letter "G" in "God" with the lowercase letter "g." This change in the Jehovah Witness Bible means that Jesus is not God, but a lower god; and, therefore, Jesus should not be worshiped as God. Read Philippians 2:5-11.

Let's look at a few more examples:

Colossians 1:16-17 (KJV)
16 For by him were all things created, that are in heaven, and that are in earth, visible and invisible, whether they be thrones, or dominions, or principalities, or powers: all things were created by him, and for him: 17 And he is before all things, and by him all things consist.

Colossians 1:16-17 (Jehovah Witness Bible—NWT)
16 Because by means of him all other things were created in the heavens and on the earth, the things visible and the things invisible, whether they are thrones or lordships or governments or authorities. All other things have been created through him and for him. 17 Also, he is before all other things, and by means of him all other things were made to exist.

The KJV says that all things were created by Jesus (stating that He is The Creator) and that He is before all things. The Jehovah Witness Bible (NWT) says that all "other" things were created by Jesus and all "other" things were made to exist—not all things. According to the NWT, Jesus was a created being and therefore, He cannot be The Creator, as it says in the KJV. Here again, any inserts or deletions changes the entire meaning.

In Revelation the Jehovah Witness Bible, changes the case in "King" and "Lord." The meaning of this is that Christ is Lord of only the lower "lords." In the King James Version, Christ is Lord of all Lords and King of all Kings—meaning there is nothing or no one else above Him.

Revelation 19:16 (KJV)
And he hath on his vesture and on his thigh a name written, KING OF KINGS, AND LORD OF LORDS.

Revelation 19:16 (NWT)
On his outer garment, yes, on his thigh, he has a name written, King of kings and Lord of lords.

The removal of these words, changing letters, and adding words is significant. The entire message of the Bible is based on the truths that Jesus is The Creator, Jesus is Lord of Lords, and Jesus is God. And this is consistent with one of the earlier Translations in Greek that dates back to 45 – 100 AD.

God warns against changing His Word.

Revelation 22:18 (KJV)
For I testify unto every man that heareth the words of the prophecy of this book, If any man shall add unto these things, God shall add unto him the plagues that are written in this book.

Questions for Discussion:

4. What did you observe about the KJV and NWT?

5. Has your view to compare versions as you study Scripture changed? If so, how?

6. Would you consider the Jehovah Witness Bible to be a translation or another religious belief? Explain.

7. Who or what would motivate someone to change Scripture, and why?

8. Do you believe it's important to understand what other religions believe? If so, why?

Reflection:

When people ask me to identify my hero, I say it's my father. He gave me the best advice: to study the Word of God for myself. I've had conversations with people—and even heard preachers—explain something from the Bible that was either untrue or misinterpreted.

As my father encouraged me, so I encourage you to study Scripture for yourself, compare the earlier versions, and be careful not to read into something based on other people's interpretations. Let Scripture interpret Scripture.

Over the thousands of years since the Bible was written in its ancient Hebrew language, some have said and others will continue to claim that God gave them a new revelation, which led them to change Scripture. This would mean that God is not all-powerful or all-knowing, and it would mean that He makes mistakes. If this is true, how can we trust that God is the Creator who is all-knowing and all-powerful? God would therefore have to be reduced to a lower level and we would have to conclude that there is no supreme being.

However, we can be sure that God is The Supreme Creator. Elohim is perfect in all His ways and thoughts, and we can trust that what He inspired thousands of years ago, can stand the test of time.

> 2 Timothy 3:16 (New Catholic Bible—NCB)
> *All Scripture is inspired by God and is useful for teaching, for refutation, for correction, and for training in uprightness.*

Questions for Further Study:

- Why should we compare translations and/or other beliefs?
- What are other translations and transliterations of the Bible, and when were they published?
- What are the Dead Sea Scrolls?
- What additional insights have you learned from this lesson?

Your Reflections:

Additional responses to questions and/or notes:

LESSON 4

JOHN THE BAPTIST: AN OVERVIEW OUTLINE

Now that we have spent time learning about the importance of Bible study; prayer, praise, and worship; and various translations of the Bible, we now transition to our lessons on the life of John the Baptist. Below is a list of books in the Bible, and its chapters and verses where John the Baptist is mentioned. Remember to always approach Scripture first by praying for guidance and clarity from The Holy Spirit.

Read each verse and the entire chapter of Luke 1, for an overview of the life of John the Baptist. If you are studying a different topic or person, this same principle can be applied. For example, if you were studying the book of John, start by first reading through the entire book.

This list is in chronological order. It will help as we gain insight into the life of John the Baptist, and an example of how to do an in-depth study of Scripture.

Book	*Chapter*	*Verse(s)*
Isaiah	40	3-5
Malachi	3	1
	4	5-6
Luke	1	1-80
	3	1-20
Matthew	3	1-17
	11	2-19
	14	1-12
	16	13-14
Mark	1	1-11
	6	14-29
	8	27-28
John	1	6-37
	3	23-36
	4	1
	5	31-36
	10	40-42
Acts	1	4-5
	11	15-16
	19	4-6

A Chronological Outline of John's Life:

John's Godly Parents
- Luke 1:5-10
  - Zacharias (or in other translations, Zachariah) was a priest who served in the Temple
  - Elizabeth was married to Zacharias; she was a daughter of Aaron (from the priestly line of Levi—Exodus 4:14)
  - Zacharias and Elizabeth were both righteous before God
  - They were old and had no children
  - Herod was king of Judea

John's birth is announced by the Angel Gabriel
- Luke 1:11-16
  - An angel of God appeared to Zacharias
  - Zacharias was fearful when he saw the angel
  - The angel told Zacharias that his prayers were answered, he would have a son, and his name would be John
  - John
    - Would give great joy and gladness to his parents
    - Would have many rejoice at his birth
    - Would be great in the sight of God
    - Would not drink strong drink or wine
    - Would be filled with The Holy Spirit in the womb
    - Would turn many of the children of Israel to Elohim

Prophesies about John and the Old Testament Prophet, Elijah (who prepares The Way)
- Isaiah 40:3-5; Malachi 3:1 and 4:5-6; Matthew 3:3 and 11:14; Mark 1:1-3; Luke 1:17; and John 1:6-8
  - A messenger will be sent and prepare the people for the coming of the Lord
  - John is Elijah
  - John is a voice shouting in the wilderness
  - John would go before Jesus in the spirit and power of Elias

Zacharias doubts and cannot speak
- Luke 1:18-23
  - Zacharias doubts they could have a child because of their age
  - The angel tells Zacharias his position and name:
    - The angel's name is Gabriel
    - Gabriel stands in the presence of God
    - Gabriel was sent by Elohim to bring good news to Zacharias
  - Zacharias' unbelief resulted in him being unable to speak until his son was born
  - The people waiting outside see that Zacharias cannot speak and believe that he must have seen a vision

<u>Elizabeth is pregnant & rejoices</u>
- Luke 1:24-25

<u>Gabriel announces the birth of The Messiah</u>
- Luke 1:26-38
  - When Elizabeth was six months pregnant, God sent the angel Gabriel to a virgin named Mary
  - Mary was engaged to Joseph, who was a descendant of King David
  - Gabriel tells Mary that she has found favor with the Lord and will give birth to a son
  - Mary's son would be named Jesus
  - Jesus would be great, and the Son of the Most High
  - Jesus's kingdom would never end
  - Gabriel says "nothing is impossible with God"

<u>Mary visits Elizabeth and praises God</u>
- Luke 1:39-56
  - At the sound of Mary's greeting, Elizabeth's child leaped within her
  - Elizabeth acknowledges that Mary is the mother of her Lord
  - Mary praises God

<u>John is born</u>
- Luke 1:57-66
  - Elizabeth gives birth to a son
  - Family and neighbors rejoice
  - John is circumcised
  - Zacharias speaks
  - News spread and people knew that God was with John in a special way

<u>Zacharias prophesies and praises God</u>
- Luke 1:67-79
  - Zacharias was filled with The Holy Spirit
  - Zacharias' praise and prophecy
    - God has visited and redeemed His people
    - A Savior has been sent from the royal line of David
    - The Israelites would be saved from their enemies and all who hate them
    - God remembered his covenant to Abraham
    - They can serve Elohim without fear
    - His son has been chosen to prepare the way for The Lord
    - God is merciful

John's description & preparation for Public Ministry
- Luke 1:80; Matthew 3:1; Matthew 3:4; and Mark 1:6
  - John grew and became strong in The Spirit
  - John lived in the wilderness until his public ministry to Israel
  - John ate locust and wild honey

John's Ministry of Baptism and Repentance
- Matthew 3:2; Matthew 3:5-12; Mark 1:4-5; and Luke 3:1-20
  - John began preaching about repentance and turning to God
  - John said that the Kingdom of Heaven is near
  - John confronts the Pharisees and Sadducees
  - John talks about good fruit, bad fruit, and God's judgment

John Baptizes The Messiah
- Matthew 3:13-17 and Mark 1:9-11
  - John declares that Jesus is greater than him
  - John baptizes Jesus
  - The Spirit of God descended like a dove on Jesus

Jesus and John clarify their positions and ministry
- Mark 1:7; John 1:14-37; John 3:23-36; and John 5:31-36
  - John lets his disciples know that he is not The Messiah
  - John says that Jesus must become greater while he becomes less
  - John confirms that Jesus is sent by God, and is The Son of God
  - John talks about how to have eternal life—through The Messiah
  - Jesus is baptizing more people than John
  - Jesus tells people that He has a greater ministry than John

John is in prison
- Matthew 11:2; Matthew 14:3-5; and Mark 6:17-20
  - John speaks truth to power
  - John is imprisoned by Herod

Jesus confirms that He is The Messiah and talks about John
- Matthew 11:2-13
  - John asks Jesus if He is The Messiah
  - Jesus responds with His evidence of miracles
    - The blind see
    - The lame walk
    - The lepers are cured
    - The deaf hear
    - The dead are raised to life
    - The Good News is being preached to the poor

Jesus describes John
- Matthew 11:7-19
  - John is the messenger, sent to prepare the way, for The Messiah
  - Jesus is greater than John
  - John is Elijah
  - John did not spend time eating or drinking (strong drink)
  - People said he was possessed by a demon

John is killed
- Matthew 14:6-12 and Mark 6:21-29
  - John is killed in prison by Herod and his family
  - John's disciples bury him

People think Jesus is John the Baptist
- Matthew 14:1-2 and 16:13-14; Mark 6:14-16 and 8:27-28
  - Herod thinks Jesus is John raised from the dead
  - Some people think Jesus is John the Baptist

People believed in Jesus
- John 10:40-42
  - People believed in John's message

John's Baptism & Jesus' Baptism
- Matthew 3:11; Mark 1:8; Acts 1:4-5; 11:15-16; and 19:4-6
  - Jesus reminds His disciples that John baptized with water and they would be baptized with The Holy Spirit
  - Peter remembers Jesus' words and talks about John's baptism
  - Paul talks about John's baptism, which called for repentance

Questions for Discussion:

1. How would you explain the story of John the Baptist?

2. How does this overview prepare you for the study of John?

Reflection:

Over the years I have had a number of conversations about the meaning of a particular verse. Scripture should be interpreted with an understanding of the context of the verse and its surrounding chapters, as well as a comparison of other verses in the Bible. Teachers and/or Bible scholars may say the Bible means one thing or another and it's accepted as truth. However, there may be no Biblical information or basis found in their conclusion(s). While this reflection repeats what has been mentioned previously, it is intended to convey how important it is for you to stay in The Word of God and rely on the power of The Holy Spirit, to give you understanding and wisdom.

Questions for Further Study:

- How should we approach Scripture?
- What is the main theme of the life of John the Baptist?
- How would an outline of a topic be helpful?
- What insights have you learned from this lesson?

Your Reflections:

Additional responses to questions and/or notes:

LESSON 5

JOHN'S PARENTS & HIS BIRTH ANNOUNCEMENT
Read Luke 1:5-14

In this lesson we will learn about the origin of John's name, his parents, and the foreign rulers during his time.

John's parents, Zechariah and Elizabeth were godly and from a priestly lineage. They were old in age and had no children.

One day while Zechariah was serving in his priestly role, an angel appeared and told him that his prayers were heard and that he would have a son.

> Luke 1:13 (NLT)
> *But the angel said, "Don't be afraid, Zechariah! God has heard your prayer. Your wife, Elizabeth, will give you a son, and you are to name him John.*

Questions for Discussion:

1. How would a righteous married couple be an example to others?

2. Why do you think that Zachariah's prayers were not answered until many years later?

3. What do you think a child's life would be like to have godly parents even before the child is born?

John's name means grace by God or God is gracious. Although we may not know the real Hebrew name for John, how blessed he was that God Almighty would name him. What an amazing blessing that God would name your child!

A meaning for "gracious" is kind, giving, and one who receives undeserved favor and mercy from God. John was sent to tell of God's coming grace—His Son, Jesus.

John and Jesus were born when Herod was the king of Judah. It was during a time of Greek influence and the Roman rule of Egypt and Jerusalem.

Luke 1:14 continues with the angel telling Zechariah that people will have joy and gladness because of John's birth.

Questions for Discussion:

4. Why do you think names are important to God?

5. Have you ever wanted to change your name? If so, why and what would it be?

6. What do you think it was like for the Hebrews to live under the control of a foreign nation?

Reflection:

In this lesson we see that God named John. His name reflected a loving characteristic of our Mighty Creator. Imagine being given a name that has a blessing or a prayer attached to it. Imagine changing your name or using a nickname to reflect the person God wants you to be and/or a gift He has given you. Imagine how it might influence the way you thought or lived.

I've often wondered what was the ancient Hebrew name for God and Jesus. It is something that I continue to research. **YAHWEH** gave us His (real) name and a *"name for all generations to use,"* but because of the evil hearts of men, it has either been lost or hidden.

> Exodus 3:15 (Names of God Bible—NOG)
> *15 Again Elohim said to Moses, "This is what you must say to the people of Israel: Yahweh Elohim of your ancestors, the Elohim of Abraham, Isaac, and Jacob, has sent me to you. This is my name forever. This is my title throughout every generation.*

Questions for Further Study:

- How significant can the meaning of a name have?
- Why was Herod the king of Judah?
- When did people start calling John, "John the Baptist?"
- When did the Romans conquer and rule Egypt and Jerusalem?
- What insights have you learned from this lesson?

Your Reflections:

Additional Responses to questions and/or notes:

LESSON 6

NAMES OF GOD

When studying Scripture, there are times the journey will lead you in an unexpectedly enlightening direction. In the previous lesson, we saw that God Himself named John. Throughout Scripture, names carry deep meaning and significance. God often renamed or gave names to individuals—such as Abraham, Sarah, and Jacob; and Jesus renamed Simon to Peter. These moments were not arbitrary; they marked identity, purpose, and divine calling.

In this lesson, we will explore the names of God, Jesus, and The Holy Spirit. As we examine the following verses that reference their Hebrew names, it's important to understand that there is ongoing discussion—and in some cases, missing historical information—regarding the original or "true" name of our Creator.

> Exodus 3:13-15 (Names of God Bible—NOG)
> *13 Then Moses replied to Elohim, "Suppose I go to the people of Israel and say to them, 'The Elohim of your ancestors has sent me to you,' and they ask me, 'What is his name?' What should I tell them?" 14 Elohim answered Moses, "Ehyeh Who Ehyeh. This is what you must say to the people of Israel: 'Ehyeh has sent me to you.'" 15 Again Elohim said to Moses, "This is what you must say to the people of Israel: Yahweh Elohim of your ancestors, the Elohim of Abraham, Isaac, and Jacob, has sent me to you. This is my name forever. This is my title throughout every generation.*

The last line in verse 15 says, *"This is my name forever. This is my title throughout every generation."* **YAHWEH** is giving His name and then says that it is His name for every generation to know. So what happened?

> Jeremiah 16:19-21 (NOG)
> *19 Yahweh is my strength and my fortress, my refuge in times of trouble. Nations come to you from the most distant parts of the world and say, "Our ancestors have inherited lies, worthless and unprofitable gods." 20 "People can't make gods for themselves. They aren't really gods. 21 That is what I will teach them. This time I will make my power and my strength known to them. Then they will know that my name is Yahweh."*

In Jeremiah 16:21, **YAHWEH** declares that we will know His name. If we were speaking to the ancient Hebrews and used the term "God," they wouldn't recognize who we were referring to. The word "God," as commonly used today, appears to have roots in pagan terminology and does not reflect the ancient name revealed in Scripture.

<u>Wikipedia</u>
> The English word **god** comes from the Old English god, which itself is derived from the Proto-Germanic *guđán.

<u>Jeremiah 23:27</u> (NASB)
Who intend to make My people forget my name by their dreams which they relate to one another, just as their fathers forgot My name because of Baal?

In Jeremiah 23, **YAHWEH** is saying that someone intended to make His people forget His name. This is a deliberate act of disobedience, contempt, and an evil that would result in consequences.

In the surrounding verses of Malachi 1:6, **YAHWEH** is talking about sacrifices. However, this particular verse is relevant as we continue to learn more about the use of His name.

<u>Malachi 1:6</u> (NLT)
The LORD of Heaven's Armies says to the priests: "A son honors his father, and a servant respects his master. If I am your father and master, where are the honor and respect I deserve? You have shown contempt for my name!

We honor our father or someone in authority; however, The Most High God says that we don't honor Him, but instead we show contempt for His name. Let's look at the meaning of contempt:

- The feeling that a person or a thing is beneath consideration.
- An arrogant disregard for something that should be taken into account.
- The offense of being disobedient to or disrespectful.

<u>The Britannica</u>
https://www.britannica.com/topic/religion
> After the Babylonian Exile (6th century BCE), and especially from the 3rd century BCE on, Jews ceased to use the name Yahweh for two reasons. As <u>Judaism</u> became a universal rather than merely local <u>religion</u>, the more common noun <u>Elohim</u>, meaning 'God,' tended to replace Yahweh to demonstrate the universal <u>sovereignty</u> of Israel's God over all others. At the same time, the divine name was increasingly regarded as too sacred to be uttered; it was thus replaced vocally in the <u>synagogue</u> ritual by the Hebrew word Adonai ("My Lord"), which was translated as Kyrios ("Lord") in the Septuagint, the Greek version of the <u>Hebrew Scriptures</u>.

We are told that The Messiah's name in Hebrew is **MASHIACH**, and that some of the Hebrew names for Jesus are **YAHUSHUA, YAHUSHA,** or **YESHUA**. His name was translated to Iesous Soter meaning Jesus the Savior. This is concerning because some believe that Iesous was possibly adapted from the Greek healing goddess Ieso. It is also important to note that there is no letter "J" in the Hebrew alphabet. In addition, the letter "J" was not used (or came into existence as it is known today) until between the 1400's - 1500's.

Imagine knowing and using the real name of our Creator, and how it would give us a richer experience, as well as a deeper reverence for His name. The decisions that came from mere men who knowingly or unknowingly were influenced by Satan has resulted in us not being able to "*mention His name to all generations*" (Exodus 3:15).

> Isaiah 40:17-18 (Names of God Bible—NOG)
> [17] *All the nations amount to nothing in his presence. He considers them less than nothing and worthless.* [18] *To whom, then, can you compare **El**? To what statue can you compare him?*

> Jeremiah 17:9 (KJV)
> *The heart is deceitful above all things, and desperately wicked: who can know it?*

While we have explored possible pagan origins for the names of God and Jesus, there are other sources that offers a different explanation. Following are two examples to consider:

Bible Study Tools
https://www.biblestudytools.com/bible-study/topical-studies/yeshua-deliverer-savior.html
> *In Aramaic, the term, "Yeshu," was transliterated from the Hebrew term of Yeshua, pronounced as "Yeh-shoo," and missing the "a." Greek translations have "Yeshua" listed as **YESOUS**, among first century Greeks, of which the name, Jesus is derived. The involvement of the Council of Nicea, within the Roman Catholic Church, as well as the influence of the English language into biblical text changed the use of "Yeshua" to describe the Savior into **Jesus**. "Yeshua" can be found most in the Hebrew Bible and other ancient texts that are still referenced among those in the Jewish faith. Hebrew is still considered the holy language used primarily for worshipping and prayer to God.*

Ancient Hebrew Research Center
https://www.ancient-hebrew.org/hebrew-names/from-where-did-the-name-jesus-come.htm
> *The name "Jesus" has a long, long history. The origin of this name is the Hebrew name יהושע (yehoshu'a, Strong's #3091 [Latinized as Joshua]), which means "Yahweh saves."*
>
> *When this Hebrew name was transliterated in the Greek Septuagint (2,000 year old Greek translation of the Hebrew Bible) it was written as Ἰησοῦς (iesous). The Greek alphabet had no "Y" sound, so it used the "I" sound. The Greek alphabet has no consonant "H," or equivalent, so this sound is dropped. The Greek alphabet also had no "Sh" sound, so it used the "S" sound. Then, Greek male names end with "s," so the "s" was added. And this is how יהושע (yehoshu'a) became Ἰησοῦς (iesous) in the Greek.*
>
> *It is common for names to shift and evolve when transferred from one culture to another.*

Names and words have been translated or transliterated to fit the many languages around the world for understanding. It is important to also consider that our enemy, Satan, and the legions of demons would never want us to know or to call on the real name of **YAHWEH**; they understand the power, glory, and honor in the name of The Almighty Creator.

Some of the known or commonly accepted Hebrew names for God, Jesus, and The Holy Spirit listed on the following page are from Bible translations and transliterations. I encourage you to continue to do your own study and research to discover the many names of **EL ELYON** (The Most High God).

EHAYAH, EHAYAH ASHER EHAYAH
I Am, I Am That I Am

RUACH HA'QODESH
The Holy Spirit

EL, ELOHIYM, ELOHIM, ELOAH
God

YAHUSHA, YAHUSHUA, or **YESHUA**
God Is Salvation

EL ELYON
The Most High God

YAHUSHA HA'MASHIACH
Jesus the Messiah *or* Jesus Christ

EL ROI
The God Who watches over me

YHWH, YAHWEH, YAHUAH, YAH
Lord or God

EL SHADDAI
God Almighty

YAHUAH ELOHAYNU
The Lord our God

MASHIACH
Messiah

YAHUAH ROPHE'KA
The Lord who heals you

RUACH
Spirit

YAHWEH TSEVA'OTH
The Lord of Hosts

The Creator is all-powerful, all-knowing, and omnipresent with no beginning or end. All of who **YAHWEH** is cannot possibly be contained in just one or a few names.

Scripture tells us that **YAHWEH** looks at the heart of man. Because He knows our hearts, I believe what matters most to Him is that we trust Him, call on Him, and live for Him—regardless of the specific name we know or are accustomed to using.

Questions for Discussion:

1. What difference do you think it may make to know the real name of God?

2. What do you think Jeremiah 23:27 is saying?

3. How might "the rulers of the darkness of this world" benefit from us not knowing the real name of our Creator? See Ephesians 6:12.

4. How would you explain Jeremiah 17:9-10 as it relates to this lesson?

5. Do you feel that God's Hebrew name should be considered? Explain.

Reflection:

My father and mother called on God and relied on The Holy Spirit. They believed in Jesus and trusted in His promises. Both went to be with the Lord in 2005, just five months apart from each other. I can imagine them now in paradise, knowing and praising the true name of **YAHUAH ELOHAYHEM** (The Lord their God). I have continued to pray and ask **YAHWEH** to reveal truths about His names and their meanings. **EL ELYON** (The Most High God) knows our heart and He hears our prayers no matter what name we feel led to call Him, or what we know His name to be. **YAHUAH ELOHAYNU** (The Lord our God) love us, and deeply wants us to have a relationship with Him.

Questions for Further Study:

- What are other Hebrew names for Jesus?
- What are other explanations about the origin for the name of "God"?
- What are other names and meaning of **YHWH**?
- What insights have you learned from this lesson?

Your Reflections:

Additional responses to questions and/or notes:

LESSON 7

THE PRESENCE OF THE HOLY SPIRIT
Luke 1:15 & John 14:16-26

In this lesson we will discuss The Holy Spirit, and how John was filled with The Spirit in his mother's womb.

Before Jesus left the earth, He told His disciples that The Father would send The Holy Spirit. Read John 14:16-26. The Holy Spirit is daily guiding those who have given their life to Christ. He speaks to our spirit through His Word (the Bible), through others, and through our dreams. Although we have talents, skills, and abilities, it is only The Holy Spirit who gives spiritual gifts to the followers of Jesus. These gifts are used to help us in our relationship and service to The Lord and to one another.

The following reference was used to help give direction and understanding of who is The Holy Spirit.

Bible Study Tools:
https://www.biblestudytools.com/bible-study/topical-studies/who-is-the-holy-spirit-5-things-you-need-to-know.html

The Holy Spirit was present in Creation (Genesis 1:2) and in the end (Revelations 22:17).

- The Holy Spirit is a person. *"Being a person, The Holy Spirit has feelings. He can become sad or angry, and others can insult Him and blaspheme against Him."* Read the following verses:

    Isaiah 63:10
    Matthew 12:31
    Acts 7:51
    Ephesians 4:30
    Hebrews 10:29

- *"He has intentions, shows willfulness and discretion, loves, communicates, testifies, teaches, and prays. These are qualities that distinguish Him as a person."* Read the following verses:

    Nehemiah 9:20
    John 15:26
    Acts 13:2
    Romans 8:26-27 and 15:30
    1 Corinthians 12:11

- *"The Holy Spirit was present during each stage of Christ's life."*

  <u>Luke 1:35</u> (KJV)
  And the angel answered and said unto her, The Holy Ghost shall come upon thee, and the power of the Highest shall overshadow thee: therefore also that holy thing which shall be born of thee shall be called the Son of God.

  <u>Matthew 3:16</u> (NASB)
  After He was baptized, Jesus came up immediately from the water; and behold, the heavens were opened, and He saw the Spirit of God descending as a dove and settling on Him.

- *"The Holy Spirit works in the lives of believers."* Read John 14:16-17.

- *"The Holy Spirit works in the world through evangelism."* Read John 16:8 and Acts 1:7-8.

Questions for Discussion:

1. Who is The Holy Spirit and what does He do?

2. How has The Holy Spirit worked in your life?

John and his mother were filled with **RUACH HA'QODESH** (The Holy Spirit).

  <u>Luke 1:15</u> (NLT)
  For he will be great in the eyes of the Lord. He must never touch wine or other alcoholic drinks. He will be filled with the Holy Spirit, even before his birth.

  <u>Luke 1:41</u> (AMP)
  When Elizabeth heard Mary's greeting, her baby leaped in her womb; and Elizabeth was filled with the Holy Spirit and empowered by Him.

In Luke, as well as in other Bible verses, an unborn child was considered fully human with a mind, body, and spirit. These precious children can suck their thumb, smile, and feel pain. Read Psalm 139:13-16.

Read the following verses and discuss some of the gifts from The Holy Spirit:

Romans 12:6-8
1 Corinthians 12:1-11
1 Peter 4:10-11
Acts 2:1-41

In addition, other gifts have been identified that are referred to as the "Seven Gifts of The Holy Spirit," meaning that The Spirit gives these gifts: wisdom, understanding, counsel, fortitude, knowledge, piety, and fear of The Lord.

John would have wisdom, understanding, the ability to counsel, knowledge, and the fear of The Lord. He would have fortitude, which means strength of mind that enables a person to encounter danger or bear pain or adversity with courage.

Questions for Discussion:

3. Why do you think John would not have strong drinks?

4. Have you ever given up something? If so, explain and how has it helped you?

5. What do you think it meant when Luke 1:15 said that John would be filled with The Holy Spirit while he was in the womb?

6. What are your spiritual gifts and how have you been able to use them?

7. What does piety mean?

There are a number of spiritual gift tests you can take. I encourage you to learn more about the gifts that **RUACH HA'QODESH** (The Holy Spirit) has given so that you can more fully serve our Mighty Creator and Savior.

Reflection:

While working at a local newspaper in the human resource department, I walked by a man who came to interview for a job. I immediately felt a sense of violence about him and talked with some of my colleagues about the applicant. They spoke highly of him and how professionally dressed he was for the interview. When I reviewed his application, I noticed that he had served time in prison because of gang violence. Everyone in the office was shocked. I was in my early 20's at the time, but I didn't understand where that feeling (or voice in my spirit) came from. It wasn't until several years later that I would learn about spiritual gifts and discover that one of the gifts that The Holy Spirit had given me was discernment. This awareness continues to guide me as I try to make decisions that are led by The Holy Spirit.

Questions for Further Study:

- What spiritual gifts has The Holy Spirit given to the followers of Jesus?
- How do our spiritual gifts work with one another?
- What is the difference between a talent or skill and a spiritual gift?
- What insights have you learned from this lesson?

Your Reflections:

Additional responses to questions and/or notes:

LESSON 8

BODY, SOUL, & SPIRIT

In Lesson 7 we discussed The Holy Spirit and we touched on some of the gifts from The Spirit. In this Lesson, we will take a look at how God has given us three (3) distinctive parts and how they work together: 1) our body, 2) our soul, and 3) our spirit. In addition, we will look at the supernatural spiritual world.

> I Thessalonians 5:23 (NLT)
> *Now may the God of peace make you holy in every way, and may your whole spirit and soul and body be kept blameless until our Lord Jesus Christ comes again.*

> Matthew 10:28 (NLT)
> *Don't be afraid of those who want to kill your body; they cannot touch your soul. Fear only God, who can destroy both soul and body in hell.*

Our body is the physical part of what we can see.

The following references were used to help give further guidance in understanding the body, soul, and spirit.

Bibles for America Blog:
https://blog.biblesforamerica.org/the-three-parts-of-man-spirit-soul-and-body
https://blog.biblesforamerica.org/difference-between-soul-and-spirit

Christianity.com:
https://www.christianity.com/wiki/salvation/difference-between-a-soul-and-a-spirit.html

Our Body
The **body** as our external part is the outer organ, possessing world-consciousness, that we may contact the material world. The body contains the soul, and the soul is the vessel that contains the spirit.

Through its five senses, **our body** exists in and contacts the tangible things of the material world. It's the visible, external part of our being. Our soul is contained in our body, and our soul is the vessel containing our spirit.

Our Soul
Our soul is our personality, who we are. With our soul we think, reason, consider, remember, and wonder. We experience emotions like happiness, love, sorrow, anger, relief, and compassion. And we're able to resolve, choose, and make decisions.

Ezekiel 18:4 (NCB)
Do not forget that all lives are mine. The life of the father and the life of the son are both mine. Only the person who sins shall die.

Read the story about the rich man and Lazarus in Luke 16:19-31.

Questions for Discussion:

1. What is the conversation the rich man is having with Abraham?

2. What do you notice about Lazarus and the rich man's soul?

3. Where is the rich man's physical body after his death?

4. Based on this story, what do you think you will experience after life on this earth?

Bibles for America Blog (continued):
https://blog.biblesforamerica.org/the-three-parts-of-man-spirit-soul-and-body

Our Spirit and The Spirit
*"In the **spirit,** God as the Spirit dwells; in the **soul,** our self dwells; and in the body, the physical senses dwell. God sanctifies us, **first,** by taking possession of our **spirit** through regeneration (John 3:5-6); **second,** by spreading Himself as the life-giving Spirit from our spirit into our **soul** to saturate and transform our soul (Romans 12:2; and 2 Corinthians 3:18); and **last,** by enlivening our mortal **body** through our soul (Romans 8:11, 13) and transfiguring our body by His life power (Philippians 3:21)."*

*"God's intention concerning us, is that we would **contain** and **express** Him. But to express God, we need to be filled with Him. When we believed in Jesus Christ, we received Him and were regenerated, or born again, in our spirit."*

Read and discuss the following verses:

John 3:5-6
Romans 12:2
II Corinthians 3:18
Romans 8:11-17
Philippians 3:21

1 Corinthians 2:14 (New Catholic Bible—NCB)
An unspiritual person refuses to accept what pertains to the Spirit of God, for to him such things are foolish. He is unable to understand them because they can be discerned only in a spiritual way.

1 Corinthians 2:14 (NIV)
The person without the Spirit does not accept the things that come from the Spirit of God but considers them foolishness, and cannot understand them because they are discerned only through the Spirit.

1 Corinthians 2:14 (NLT)
But people who aren't spiritual can't receive these truths from God's Spirit. It all sounds foolish to them and they can't understand it, for only those who are spiritual can understand what the Spirit means.

Questions for Discussion:

5. Who gives birth to spiritual life?

6. How do we know if we belong to God?

7. Why is it hard to talk about the things of The Spirit with just anyone?

There are other spirits involved who are part of the supernatural world. The following reference was used to provide information on these other spirits:

The Gospel Coalition:
https://www.thegospelcoalition.org/essay/the-spirit-world-angels/

The term "angels" refers to spiritual beings who were created by God before the world was created for the purposes of worshiping him and accomplishing his will. Angels were given the ability to choose whether to follow God's will and to obey his commands, and a certain faction followed Satan in his rebellion against the Lord. In the New Testament, these rebellious angels are referred to most commonly as "demons" or "unclean spirits."

Read the following verses about the Angels of The Lord of Hosts:

Nehemiah 9:6
Genesis 28:12
Psalm 103:20
2 Samuel 14:20
Exodus 33:2

Read the entire chapter of Job 1.

Ephesians 6:12 (New Catholic Bible—NCB)
For we are not struggling against flesh and blood, but against the principalities, the powers, and the cosmic rulers of this present darkness, and against the spirits of evil in the heavens.

Ephesians 6:12 (NLT)
For we are not fighting against flesh-and-blood enemies, but against evil rulers and authorities of the unseen world, against mighty powers in this dark world, and against evil spirits in the heavenly places.

Questions for Discussion:

8. Why did God create Angels?

9. What do you notice about Satan in Job 1?

10. Who can communicate to our spirit and direct our actions? Explain how this influences our lives.

11. What is the difference between spirits and The Holy Spirit?

12. Why would it be important to be careful about who or what you listen to, what you read, and what you watch?

13. Do you believe that the supernatural world can take on a physical form? Explain.

John the Baptist had The Spirit in him before he was born! He had a deep spiritual connection to God in the womb. When you accept Jesus The Messiah, The Holy Spirit guides and comforts you. Read John 14:16-26.

Read James 2:19-26 and notice who believes in God.

There is a difference between someone who simply believes and someone who is led by The Holy Spirit and follows the example of Jesus.

Matthew 7:21-23 (KJV)
21 Not every one that saith unto me, Lord, Lord, shall enter into the kingdom of heaven; but he that doeth the will of my Father which is in heaven. 22 Many will say to me in that day, Lord, Lord, have we not prophesied in thy name? and in thy name have cast out devils? and in thy name done many wonderful works? 23 And then will I profess unto them, I never knew you: depart from me, ye that work iniquity.

<u>Matthew 7:21-23</u> (NLT)

21 "Not everyone who calls out to me, 'Lord! Lord!' will enter the Kingdom of Heaven. Only those who actually do the will of my Father in Heaven will enter. 22 On judgment day many will say to me, 'Lord! Lord! We prophesied in your name and cast out demons in your name and performed many miracles in your name. 23 But I will reply, 'I never knew you. Get away from me, you who break God's laws.'

Jesus doesn't say that I knew you once and you lost your salvation, but rather He says, I never knew you—meaning—at no point in time did I ever know you.

Let's look at another example in Revelation:

<u>Revelation 21:7-8</u> (NASB)

7 The one who overcomes will inherit these things, and I will be his God and he will be My son. 8 But for the cowardly, and unbelieving, and abominable, and murderers, and sexually immoral persons, and sorcerers, and idolaters, and all liars, their part will be in the lake that burns with fire and brimstone, which is the second death."

<u>Questions for Discussion:</u>

14. What's the difference between a believer and a follower of Jesus?

15. What insights have you learned from James 2:19-26; Matthew 7:21-23; John 14:21-24; and Revelation 21:7-8?

<u>Reflection:</u>

In my father's twenties, he worked as a maintenance manager at a Jewish Synagogue. During one of his breaks, he went into the library and heard a voice speak to his spirit and say "why don't you read the Bible, you've never read that before." While reading, he was thinking about how foolish these writings were. Although The Holy Spirit was not living within my father, God spoke to his spirit and prompted my dad to read the Bible.

Many years later when he was driving his taxi cab and picked up a female passenger, she asked him if he knew Jesus. My dad thought to himself "not another religious nut." As she started talking to my dad about The Lord, his heart opened to The Truth.

> John 14:6 (KJV)
> *"Jesus said to him, I am the way, the truth, and the life. No one comes to the Father except through Me."*

The woman prayed with my father and he received Christ as his personal Savior. As she left his taxi, she gave my dad a Bible. The Holy Spirit spoke through this woman, and that day my father's life changed for all eternity.

Years later, he remembered the thoughts he had when he read the Bible for the first time, when he was a natural man:

> 1 Corinthians 2:14 (KJV)
> *But the natural man receiveth not the things of the Spirit of God: for they are foolishness unto him: neither can he know them, because they are spiritually discerned.*

My dad was now spiritually alive in Christ because of his belief—which results in actions. Later, my dad would share The Gospel with others. He impacted the life of his wife, Lucille and their six children (my five brothers and me), including many others; who continue to carry his legacy of faith and the importance of studying the Bible.

Questions for Further Study:

- What is the role of the body, soul, and spirit?
- Can you be a follower of Jesus without The Holy Spirit living in you?
- How do The Holy Spirit and other spirits work?
- Do you believe a Spirit has impacted your life? If so, how, and what Spirit?
- What insights have you learned from this lesson?

Your Reflections:

Additional responses to questions and/or notes:

LESSON 9

THE SPIRIT OF ELIJAH
Luke 1:17

As we are more than halfway through this study, let's take a look at how we are learning to do an in-depth study of Scripture:

- Understanding the importance of prayer, praise, and worship
- Reading verses where our subject/topic—John the Baptist—is mentioned
- Carefully examining Scripture verses, and comparing various translations
- Embracing and/or considering the names of God
- Researching additional information from other sources
- Gaining insights into the power of The Holy Spirit and how the spirit world works

Studying Scripture allows us to learn how to live for Christ, and helps us grow in our faith and understanding of The Most High God.

The only One that has all knowledge, understanding, wisdom, and power is God Almighty. No matter how much someone studies or how many credentials they have, Bible study is a lifetime journey. The power of The Holy Spirit can give anyone understanding and wisdom.

Let's continue with our study and introduce Elijah (in some versions his name is Elias), and see what he has to do with John the Baptist.

Elijah was an Old Testament prophet who lived around the time of the 9th Century (900 BC). It was prophesied that Elijah would come back again to prepare the way for the coming Messiah. In Matthew 11:14, Jesus says that John was Elijah (Elias). Read Matthew 11:1-19.

Throughout the Old Testament there are prophecies about the coming of The Messiah. The Bible talks about the messenger, who will come before The Messiah. Read the following verses that reference Elias and John the Baptist, including Luke 3:4-6.

Isaiah 40:3 (NLT)
Listen! It's the voice of someone shouting, "Clear the way through the wilderness for the LORD! Make a straight highway through the wasteland for our God!

Malachi 3:1 (NASB)
"Behold, I am sending My messenger, and he will clear a way before Me. And the Lord, whom you are seeking, will suddenly come to His temple; and the messenger of the covenant, in whom you delight, behold, He is coming," says the LORD of armies.

<u>Malachi 4:5-6</u> (AMP)
"Behold, I am going to send you Elijah the prophet before the coming of the great and terrible day of the LORD. He will turn the hearts of the fathers to their children, and the hearts of the children to their fathers [a reconciliation produced by repentance], so that I will not come and strike the land with a curse [of complete destruction]."

<u>Luke 1:17</u> (KJV)
And he shall go before him in the spirit and power of Elias, to turn the hearts of the fathers to the children, and the disobedient to the wisdom of the just; to make ready a people prepared for the Lord.

<u>Luke 1:17</u> (AMP)
It is he who will go as a forerunner before Him in the spirit and power of Elijah, to turn the hearts of the fathers back to the children, and the disobedient to the attitude of the righteous [which is to seek and submit to the will of God]—in order to make ready a people [perfectly] prepared [spiritually and morally] for the Lord.

Questions for Discussion:

1. Why was it important to have prophecies about The Messiah?

2. Why didn't John just come without a reference to Elijah?

3. When did Isaiah's ministry start and why may this be important?

4. What do you think it means that John had the spirit of Elias? Were they the same person?

5. Who and what do we have to prepare us for the return of our Savior, Jesus?

Elijah/Elias

The short and impactful story of Elijah starts in 1 Kings 17:1. Elijah seems to come from out of nowhere and yet speaks with the kings of Israel and Judah. He is described as a Tishbite, who was from Gilead. In contrast, John is born at a time when the king of Jerusalem is a Roman—Herod. However, like Elijah, John confronts a king, including other leaders.

Elias confronts Ahab who was the king of Israel. Ahab and his wife Jezebel were wicked in the sight of The Lord. Jezebel was a Sidonian—of Canaanite lineage (a descendant of Ham), who tried to kill Elijah.

The prophet Elijah performed miracles, which included raising a boy from the dead. He was ultimately taken to Heaven in a chariot of fire and horses of fire. See II Kings 2:11.

You can read more about Elias in: I Kings chapters 17, 18, 19, and 21; and II Kings chapters 1 and 2. He was a prophet when the children of Jacob separated and became two nations: Israel and Judah.

Below is a brief overview of how Israel split:

- In 1 Kings, David is an old man and his son Solomon becomes the next king of Israel.
- Solomon's heart turned from God, and followed the gods and practices of the foreign women he married.
- Solomon's sin resulted in the kingdom of Israel being split (I Kings 11).
- Only one tribe would be given to the descendants of David—Judah.
- Solomon's son, Rehoboam became king of Israel.
- Rehoboam was harsh so the people revolted and the kingdom split; he ruled only Judah.
- Solomon's servant, Jeroboam became the king of Israel.

Questions for Discussion:

6. What similarities do you see between John and Elijah?

7. What does the name Elias mean?

8. Other than Elijah, who else in the Bible did God take and/or He buried?

Reflection:

In Luke 13:31-32, Jesus reminds us that He will accomplish His purpose no matter who challenges Him. The Pharisees told him to go away because Herod wanted to kill him. But Jesus responds by calling Herod a fox—a cunning predator. Jesus understood that even the highest ruler in the land did not control His destiny; and therefore, He would continue with the mission from The Most High God.

When I consider the story of Elijah and John, it reminds me that our Heavenly Father's plan will be carried out, and nothing can stop Him. It should give us comfort in knowing that our assignment and our very own life is in the hand of God, and He tells us that He alone is God.

Matthew 10:28 (NIV), Jesus says the following:
"Do not be afraid of those who kill the body but cannot kill the soul. Rather, be afraid of The One who can destroy both soul and body in hell."

Isaiah 45:5-8 (Names of God Bible—NOG)
⁵ I am Yahweh, and there is no other. There is no other Elohim besides me. I will strengthen you, although you don't know me, ⁶ so that from the east to the west people will know that there is no Elohim except me. I am Yahweh, and there is no other. ⁷ I make light and create darkness. I make blessings and create disasters. I, Yahweh, do all these things. ⁸ Rain down from above, you heavens, and pour down righteousness, you skies. Let the earth open. Let salvation and righteousness sprout. Let them spring up. I, Yahweh, have created them.

Questions for Further Study:

- How long was the time period of Elijah until the birth of Jesus?
- Why is it necessary to make a connection with Elijah and John?
- What insights have you learned from this lesson?

Your Reflections:

Additional responses to questions and/or notes:

LESSON 10

THE MESSENGER & THE MESSIAH
Luke 1:18-79

This lesson introduces John, the coming of The Messiah, and the Angel Gabriel. Luke gives a detailed version of the announcement of John's birth, as well as the foundation and purpose of his life. Read Luke 1:18-25.

Questions for Discussion:

1. How would you describe Gabriel and his significance?

2. Why do you think God would take away Zacharias' speech?

3. What do you think was going on in Zacharias' mind in the months before and while Elizabeth was pregnant, or what would you have been thinking?

In Lesson 8 we learned about the Angels of The Lord of Hosts. Read additional information about Angels in the following verses:

Genesis 2:1
2 Samuel 14:17
Psalm 91:11
Luke 15:10
Colossians 1:16
Hebrews 1:14

In Elizabeth's sixth month of pregnancy, Gabriel appears to the virgin Mary. He tells Mary that she will have a child and He would be The Son of The Most High God. Read Luke 1:26-38.

In Luke 1:32-35, Gabriel tells Mary that the baby will be _Holy_. Only The Supreme One is Holy! Mary understood this since she called God Holy.

> Luke 1:49 (NOG)
> _Because the Almighty has done great things to me. His name is holy._

Following is a brief list of what Holy means when it refers to Jesus and God:
- Divine
- Exalted
- Sacred – worthy of respect, set apart for the worship of a Deity
- Deity – Divine status, The Creator and Supreme Being
- Worthy of complete devotion
- Perfect in goodness and righteousness

Jesus was not a mere man; He was and is The Divine. You may hear people or other religious groups describe Jesus as a prophet or a good man. However, this takes away the truth about Jesus, which denies His equality with God and that He is the only way to Elohim (John 14:6). John 1:1-16, clearly establishes the position of Jesus, including other references in Scripture.

Questions for Discussion:

4. What do you notice in Daniel 8:15-26 and Daniel 9:20-27?

5. How did Mary respond to Gabriel's message? And, how is her response significant?

6. Who else in Scripture doubted or trusted the announcement of a birth? How would you compare them to Mary and/or Zacharias?

Read Luke 1:39-56.
- Mary hurries to visit her relative Elizabeth and stays with her for three months.
- At the sound of Mary's greeting, Elizabeth's child (John) leaped within her.
- Elizabeth is joyous and honored at Mary's visit.
- Mary praises The Most High God.

Luke 1:57-79 John is born.
- Everyone rejoiced with Elizabeth and Zacharias.
- People came for the circumcision ceremony.
- After Zacharias wrote that his son's name would be John, he was able to speak.
- Zacharias, filled with The Holy Spirit, prophesied.

Questions for Discussion:

7. What do you think it was like for Mary to stay with Elizabeth? Consider their conversations.

8. How could the unborn child, John, leap for joy when he heard Mary's voice?

9. What does Mary's song of praise mean to you?

10. What do you notice about Zacharias' prophecy?

When God answers a prayer or does something that we consider special or unexpected, we should thank and praise Him. In addition, Job gives us an example of praising (honoring) God even in times of suffering. The first part of Job 13:15 (KJV) says, "*Though He slay me, yet will I trust in Him.*"

Throughout Scripture God's prophets and leaders had difficult times and suffered. In the book of Psalms, even when David was in despair and/or feared for his life, he praised **YAHWEH**.

Questions for Discussion:

11. Why should we praise God in good times as well as in difficult times? Consider what this would do for our spiritual, emotional, and mental health.

12. Read the first part of Genesis 18:14 and read Luke 1:37—How do these verses encourage you? And, what connection do you notice?

13. What are some similarities between the birth announcement of John and Jesus?

Reflection:

In Luke 1:45, Elizabeth says that Mary is blessed because she believed what The Lord said. And yet at the same time, Zacharias was blessed with a son although he did not believe. There have been many times in my life that I doubted **YAHWEH**, and yet He still answered my prayers. Other times when my prayers were not answered, I was disappointed or anxious, but I had to trust in God's goodness towards me, and that His plans were beyond my comprehension.

Isaiah 55:8-9 (KJV)
For My thoughts are not your thoughts, neither are your ways My ways, says The Lord. For as the heavens are higher than the earth, so are My ways higher than your ways and My thoughts than your thoughts.

Questions for Further Study:

- What are names of other angels in the Bible and what do they represent?
- What is the purpose of circumcising a male child on the 8th day?
- What does it mean to trust in The Most High God?
- What insights have you learned from this lesson?

Your Reflections:

Additional responses to questions and/or notes:

LESSON 11

JOHN'S PUBLIC MINISTRY
Luke 3:1-20

This Lesson covers the beginning of John's public ministry, which included baptism, repentance, and living a righteous life. It will give some insight as to how John grew up, and it's a reminder that he was set apart as a messenger to bring the Good News about Jesus, The Messiah.

> Luke 1:80 (NLT)
> *John grew up and became strong in spirit. And he lived in the wilderness until he began his public ministry to Israel.*

> Luke 1:80 (KJV)
> *And the child grew, and waxed strong in spirit, and was in the deserts till the day of his showing unto Israel.*

> Matthew 3:1 (NCB)
> *In those days, John the Baptist appeared in the desert of Judea, preaching.*

John was ready for service. He is described as one who lived in the wilderness, ate locust and honey, and wore a leather belt. Read: Matthew 3:4; Mark 1:6; and 2 Kings 1:8.

Questions for Discussion:

1. As John was growing up, what do you think it meant that he grew strong in The Spirit?

2. Why would John live in the wilderness (away from people) until his public ministry?

3. How would it change you, if for a time, you separated yourself from people and/or things that took you away from growing in The Spirit of God?

4. What was the point in mentioning John's appearance and the food he ate?

Luke 3:1 tells us who the rulers were just before John's public ministry.

One can imagine that John's time spent in the wilderness was preparation for his ministry and receiving direction from God.

> Luke 3:2 (NLT)
> *Annas and Caiaphas were the high priests. At this time a message from God came to John son of Zechariah, who was living in the wilderness.*

John's message was about confession, repentance, and preparing the way for The Messiah. Read Matthew 3:1-3 and verses 5-6; and Luke 3:3 and verses 7-20.

In Luke 3:7 John called the people "brood of vipers." He specifically calls out the Pharisees and Sadducees in Matthew:

> Matthew 3:7-12 (Amplified Bible—AMP)
> *7 But when he saw many of the Pharisees and Sadducees coming for baptism, he said to them, "You brood of vipers, who warned you to flee from the [divine] wrath and judgment to come? 8 So produce fruit that is consistent with repentance [demonstrating new behavior that proves a change of heart, and a conscious decision to turn away from sin]; 9 and do not presume to say to yourselves [as a defense], 'We have Abraham for our father [so our inheritance assures us of salvation]'; for I say to you that from these stones God is able to raise up children (descendants) for Abraham. 10 And already the axe [of God's judgment] is swinging toward the root of the trees; therefore every tree that does not bear good fruit is cut down and thrown into the fire. 11 "As for me, I baptize you with water because of [your] repentance [that is, because you are willing to change your inner self—your old way of thinking, regret your sin and live a changed life], but He (the Messiah) who is coming after me is mightier [more powerful, more noble] than I, whose sandals I am not worthy to remove [even as His slave]; He will baptize you [who truly repent] with the Holy Spirit and [you who remain unrepentant] with fire (judgment). 12 His winnowing fork is in His hand, and He will thoroughly clear out His threshing floor; and He will gather His wheat (believers) into His barn (kingdom), but He will burn up the chaff (the unrepentant) with unquenchable fire."*

"Brood of snakes" is the term used in the New Living Translation (NLT) describing these religious leaders. The King James Version (KJV) calls them a "generation of vipers." The following description of "vipers" provides us with an insight into the character of these evil leaders:

- Brood – family of snakes capable of producing venom
- Venom is a poison that is (actively delivered)—injected into its prey
- Venom – a spiteful malicious feeling or state of mind: extreme ill will
- Malicious – (intending) to do harm

Questions for Discussion:

5. Why is repentance important?

6. Based on how John described the Pharisees and Sadducees, how would you describe them and their purpose?

7. What lesson can you learn from the description of the Pharisees and Sadducees in our modern times?

8. Why did John announce the Good News, along with the coming judgment?

9. Read Matthew 7:15-27; Luke 3:8-14; James 2:14-26 (AMP version); and John 14:15. How do these verses relate to Matthew 3:7-10? Explain faith and works.

John's message was consistent with the message of Jesus —living right and helping the poor.

John was not afraid to speak out against leadership. Luke 3:19-20, informs us that Herod had many sins.

Questions for Discussion:

10. Where else in the Bible does it talk about helping the poor? And why do you think this is important to God?

11. Have you ever publicly spoken out against wicked leadership? And/or has your opinion changed about the need to speak out against sin?

12. Why would **ELOHIYM** want us to call out sinful leaders?

13. Why mention that Herod had many sins?

14. What do you think the difference is between a "sinner saved by grace" and a sinner who has not given their life to The Lord? Read 1 John 1:9 and Ephesians 2:8.

Reflection:

There's a saying, "birds of a feather flock together," meaning people with similar mindsets or behaviors tend to associate with one another. Think about the people you spend time with—do they strengthen you spiritually and help you grow, or do they pull you away from your faith? Do they encourage your walk with The Lord, or do they lead you in a different direction?

> 2 Corinthians 6:14-15 (AMP)
> [14] *Do not be unequally bound together with unbelievers [do not make mismatched alliances with them, inconsistent with your faith]. For what partnership can righteousness have with lawlessness? Or what fellowship can light have with darkness?* [15] *What harmony can there be between Christ and Belial (Satan)? Or what does a believer have in common with an unbeliever?*

Even followers of Jesus who are immature in their faith can hinder your growth—unless you are the one leading, encouraging, and discipling them.

Another example is the Pharisees, who were the religious leaders during the time of John the Baptist and Jesus. They outwardly appeared godly but were hypocrites whose hearts were far from God. Similarly, today, some priests, pastors, ministers, or teachers knowingly act in ways that contradict true godliness and lead others away from truth. Just as people back then held onto the Pharisees' words, many today rely solely on others' interpretations. But with God's Word so accessible, we have the opportunity to study Scripture ourselves and avoid being misled.

Questions for Further Study:

- What are other verses that compare faith and works?
- Do we have our own modern day Pharisees? Explain.
- What happens when you or our culture ignore sin? Consider Luke 3:19-20.
- What insights have you learned from this lesson?

Your Reflections:

Additional responses to questions and/or notes:

LESSON 12

YAHUSHA IS BAPTIZED

Baptism originates from the Greek term "baptisma." Unlike many terms we've explored in this study, it is not derived from Hebrew. Yet, in the context of the Old Testament, specifically within the Mosaic law, there exists a concept of ceremonial washing or purification mandated by God for the Israelite community. For example, read Exodus 29:4 and 30:17-21; Leviticus 15:13; and Numbers 19:1-9.

> Matthew 3:11 (AMP), John says the following:
> *"As for me, I baptize you with water because of [your] repentance [that is, because you are willing to change your inner self—your old way of thinking, regret your sin and live a changed life], but He (The Messiah) who is coming after me is mightier [more powerful, more noble] than I, whose sandals I am not worthy to remove [even as His slave]; He will baptize you [who truly repent] with the Holy Spirit and [you who remain unrepentant] with fire (judgment)."*

- John's baptism was of repentance
- Jesus baptized with The Spirit and with fire.

Matthew 3:13-17 and Mark 1:9-11 is about the baptism of Jesus. Consider that The Messiah, who is perfect, is baptized by a man.

> Matthew 3:15 (NIV) Jesus says the following:
> *"Let it be so now; it is proper for us to do this to fulfill all righteousness."*

The word righteous in Hebrew means one who <u>follows</u> the correct path, the path (way) of **ELOHIYM**. As followers of Jesus, this is what we should strive to do—follow the way of God. Read and discuss Matthew 22:36-38, and the connection with following righteousness.

Below are some suggestions as to why Jesus may have been baptized:

- To demonstrate an example of the importance of being obedient to God The Father (being righteous)
- To demonstrate a symbolic image of cleansing
- To provide a symbol of rebirth in The Spirit—a newness of our spiritual life

1. Why did John not want to baptize Jesus?

2. Why do you think **YAHUSHA** did not baptize John?

3. What is the difference between John's baptism and Jesus' baptism?

4. How would you explain Matthew 3:11? Consider what it means to be baptized with The Spirit and with fire.

Read and discuss the following verses about **RUACH HA'QODESH** (The Holy Spirit):

Matthew 3:16
Matthew 28:19
John 15:26
1 Corinthians 12:4-13
2 Corinthians 13:14
Ephesians 2:18
1 Thessalonians 1:2-5
1 Peter 1:2

After Jesus is baptized, God says He is pleased. Read Matthew 3:17 and Isaiah 42:1.

Jesus also baptized. Read John 3:22.

Questions for Discussion:

5. Why do you think God was pleased when Jesus was baptized?

6. When Jesus baptized, was it for repentance, to receive The Holy Spirit, or other reasons? Explain.

7. Does baptism alone mean that you are a follower of **YESHUA**? Explain.

8. What are three major things happening in Matthew 3:16-17?

9. What does it mean to be baptized?

10. Have your views about baptism changed? If so, how?

My father was raised Catholic, but he didn't practice Catholicism or begin reading the Bible until he accepted Jesus, as mentioned in Lesson 8. The purpose of sharing the information below from "Simply Catholic," is show how you can take a study even further and gain additional insight on various topics related to what you are studying. I found it was interesting to learn why the Catholic Church baptizes infants: https://www.simplycatholic.com/why-baptize-babies/

- *Parents bring their babies to the waters of baptism by professing a belief in Christ on behalf of the child, and promising to raise him or her in the faith. For adults who are to be baptized, the Church also requires them to profess their faith in Christ.*
- *Because baptism confers saving grace, the earlier a person comes to baptism, the better.*
- *In infant baptism, though the child is too young to have faith, the parents extend their faith on the child's behalf.*

- *On what basis does the Church believe that the faith of one person may be effective on behalf of someone else? The Scriptures are full of examples in which Jesus extends healing grace to people based on the faith of others.*
    - *For example, Jesus forgives the sins of the paralytic based on the faith of those who brought him (Matthew 9:2 and Mark 2:3-5).*
    - *Jesus heals the centurion's servant based on the faith of the centurion (Matthew 8:5-13).*
    - *Jesus exorcises the child's unclean spirit based on the father's faith (Mark 9:16-27).*
    - *We might also note that in the Old Testament, God spares the firstborn child's life during the Passover based on the parent's faith (Exodus 12:24-28).*

Reflection:

Jesus' baptism has made me consider even more the significance of being baptized. I remember being baptized because it was something you do to show that you are a follower of Jesus. I never really understood the significance or the true meaning of being immersed in water, nor did I consider the significance of Jesus being baptized.

If you have been baptized, meditate on what it means in your life. If you have not been baptized, consider your next step as a follower of Jesus.

Questions for Further Study:

- What do you think the dove symbolizes in Jesus' baptism?
- What does baptism mean to you?
- What are other examples today of being immersed in water?
- What insights have you learned from this lesson?

Your Reflections:

Additional responses to questions and/or notes:

LESSON 13

POSITIONS & POWER MADE CLEAR
Luke 3:15-18

John the Baptist and the writer of the book of John was very clear about who John the Baptist was and who the Messiah is. In this Lesson, we see how John the Baptist does not elevate himself but rather he elevates **YAHUSHA HA'MASHIACH** (Jesus The Messiah).

Mark 1:7 (NCB)
And this was the message he proclaimed: "One who is far more powerful than I am is coming after me. I am not worthy even to stoop down and loosen the straps of his sandals."

The Gospel of John was not written by John the Baptist, it was written by John, one of the 12 disciples of Jesus. This book starts with explaining who Jesus is—The Word, The Creator, and God Himself. John (the disciple) talks about John the Baptist (the messenger) who came to prepare The Way and be a witness for The Light; and this Light is, Jesus The Messiah.

John the Baptist confirms that someone is coming who is greater than him. He confirms that he is not The Messiah. Read Luke 3:15-16; John 1:1-37; and John 3:23-36.

John is making it clear as to his position and Jesus' position. In John 1:27 he says that he is unworthy to even untie the straps of Jesus' sandal. Let's review below what we learned about John the Baptist in Lessons 5 and 9:

- From a priestly line
- Godly parents
- Birth announced by the angel Gabriel
- Many rejoiced at his birth
- Great in the sight of God
- The messenger who was to go before Jesus in the spirit and power of Elijah (Elias)
- John was filled with The Holy Spirit, while in his mother's womb

John sees himself as unworthy, because he realizes who Jesus is! Do you feel worthy to be called by God? We can feel humbled, amazed, grateful, etc., but certainly not worthy.

We have read in previous lessons how faith and works fit together; John the Baptist confirms this in the following verse:

John 3:36 (NLT)
"And anyone who believes in God's Son has eternal life. Anyone who doesn't obey the Son will never experience eternal life but remains under God's angry judgment."

Questions for Discussion:

1. How does John describe Jesus in John 1:14-37?

2. Why do you think John the Baptist denied being Elias or a prophet?

3. Do you think the Pharisees cared to know who John was and who Jesus was? Why or why not? (See John 8:42-47)

4. What ways did John compare his position/status?

5. How should we personalize John 3:30 (NLT)? *"He must become greater and greater, and I must become less and less."*

Read John 5:31-36. Jesus makes it clear that what John says about Him is true, and that He has a greater witness.

Jesus says that the Scriptures point to Him:

John 5:39 (NLT)
"You search the Scriptures because you think they give you eternal life. But the Scriptures point to Me!"

Questions for Discussion:

6. Why did **YAHUSHA** say that He has "no need of human witnesses" in John 5:34?

7. In addition to John the Baptist, who else were Jesus' witnesses, and how have they influenced our lives?

Reflection:

The senior pastor at a church I attended many years ago, would begin his sermons by praying that he might decrease so that God and His Word would increase. This approach mirrored the humility exemplified by John the Baptist, offering a powerful illustration of the attitude we should adopt in relation to The Messiah. John 3:30 clearly illustrates this principle, serving as a guiding rule for how we ought to live and share the Gospel. Our lives should be an example of God's influence, casting aside our own prominence or significance in favor of a greater focus on The Divine.

Questions for Further Study:

- Why was it necessary that Jesus have a messenger?
- Who prophesied about the coming of Jesus The Messiah?
- Why do people reject Jesus?
- What insights have you learned from this lesson?

Your Reflections:

Additional responses to questions and/or notes:

LESSON 14

JOHN'S PURPOSE FULFILLED

We have reached the conclusion of John the Baptist's life story. His life started in a remarkable manner, being filled with The Holy Spirit even within his mother's womb. Although John's physical earthly life ended in tragedy, his spiritual eternal life is one of glory—a destiny that, as followers of Jesus, we will experience one day. In this lesson, we will explore John's transition from being the messenger of The Messiah to his imprisonment and execution, as well as examine those who were responsible for his death.

Herod the Great was appointed king of Judah by the Romans.
- He was king when John the Baptist was born.
- He ordered the killing of Hebrew boys from two years of age and younger, hoping to kill The Messiah. Read Matthew 2:13-18 and compare Exodus 1:15-16.

After Herod the Great's death, his kingdom was divided up by the Romans between his sister Salome I and Herod's three sons: Herod Antipas, Archelaus, and Philip.

Read Mark 6:14-20.

John the Baptist was able to speak with Herod Antipas directly because it was God Almighty's plan. If The Holy One decides, even we can speak to leaders of nations.

Herod Antipas would have known and felt the following about John:
- John's message was about repentance and The Messiah
- John had the respect of the people
- He was afraid to harm John for fear of a riot (Matthew 14:5)
- John taught about living right for God
- John was a good and holy man
- He respected John

Questions for Discussion:

1. Should we follow John's example and speak out against sin? How have things changed today?

2. How is Herodias similar to people today?

3. Why did Herod have to send soldiers to arrest John? Do you see that happening today?

4. Herod liked talking to John but still didn't take his advice. Why do you think he did not change his ways?

Read Matthew 11:2-19 and John 10:41.

While John was in prison, he sent his disciples to ask Jesus if he was The Messiah. Jesus responds as follows:
- The blind see
- The lame walk
- The lepers are cured
- The deaf hear
- The dead are raised to life
- The Good News is being preached to the poor

Questions for Discussion:

5. Why do you think John sent his disciples to ask Jesus if He was The Messiah?

6. Why do you think John did not perform miracles?

7. What did Jesus mean in Matthew 11:6 when He said that "God *blesses those who do not turn away because of Me"*?

8. Why did Jesus say that John is least in the Kingdom of Heaven?

9. How did Jesus describe John, and how can that description influence our lives?

Read Mark 6:21-29.

See below the sinful acts of Herodias that led to the murder of John:
- Rejection of God
- Rejection of righteous living
- Turned off by truth
- Imprisoned (and silenced) a man for speaking truth
- Ordered the killing of the messenger of Jesus The Messiah
- Involved her family in the murder of John the Baptist

After John's death, Herod and others think that **YESHUA** is John the Baptist raised from the dead. Read Matthew 14:1-2 and Mark 8:27-28. Other people believed John's witness about Jesus.

> John 10:40-42 (NLT)
> *"He went beyond the Jordan River near the place where John was first baptizing and stayed there awhile. And many followed him. "John didn't perform miraculous signs," they remarked to one another, "but everything he said about this man has come true." And many who were there believed in Jesus.*

Questions for Discussion:

10. Why didn't Herod just ignore the young girl's request to kill John? What lessons can we learn?

11. Why didn't John get raised from the dead?

12. Do you think you would have followed John or Jesus at that time? How can we follow their example today?

<u>The Baptism of Water and the Baptism of The Holy Spirit</u>:

Read Acts 1:4-5; 11:15-16; 19:1-7; and Mark 1:7-8.

The story of John does not end with his killing. It ends with a reminder about him being a messenger who baptized with water, and Jesus sending us The Comforter, who is, The Holy Spirit.

Questions for Discussion:

13. What pattern do you see in Mark 1:8 and in Acts 1:4-5; 11:15-16; and 19:1-7?

14. In Acts 19:1-7, how could they be called believers and not have The Holy Spirit?

15. In Acts 1:4-5, why did Jesus refer to The Holy Spirit as a gift?

16. Who is The Holy Spirit, what does He do, and what does He give?

Reflection:

As followers of Jesus we all have an assignment, and we all have The Holy Spirit living within us. Some of our assignments may not be physically or emotionally safe or end the way we want them to; however, John the Baptist was searching for eternal rewards and not temporary earthly pleasures, which do not offer lasting joy or peace. The founders of the early church (the disciples and other followers of Jesus) were looking towards the eternal.

<u>2 Timothy 4:6-8</u> (AMP)

⁶ For I am already being poured out as a drink offering, and the time of my departure [from this world] is at hand and I will soon go free. ⁷ I have fought the good and worthy and noble fight, I have finished the race, I have kept the faith [firmly guarding the Gospel against error]. ⁸ In the future there is reserved for me the [victor's] crown of righteousness [for being right with God and doing right], which the Lord, the righteous Judge, will award to me on that [great] day—and not to me only, but also to all those who have loved and longed for and welcomed His appearing.

As I meditate on 2 Timothy 4:6-8, I am reminded, as well as encouraged by the following:

- **YAHWEH** has given me an assignment.
- Jesus has given me eternal life.
- God's Spirit guides and directs my steps.
- The God who watches over me, can protect me from all harm.
- **EL ELYON** (The Most High God) is my ruler, and, The Ruler over all things.
- The Eternal God is where I find my hope and joy.

Questions for Further Study:

- How does the Baptism of John and Jesus differ?
- How far would you be willing to go for Jesus?
- What insights have you learned from this lesson?

Your Reflections:

Additional responses to questions and/or notes:

LESSON 15

REVIEW & CONCLUSION

I hope this Lesson, "*A Framework for How to Do an In-Depth Study of Scripture, Using the Life of John the Baptist*," has been helpful. Let The Holy Spirit be your guide. As you reflect on your own spiritual journey, remember that there are many ways to approach studying Scripture and growing in our relationship with The Almighty Creator.

- Love **YAHWEH** with all your heart (Mark 12:30)
- Pray daily (Colossians 4:2)
- Study the Bible (2 Timothy 2:15)
- Pray and ask The Holy Spirit for direction (John 16:13)
- Approach Scripture with humility and a teachable heart (Psalm 86:11)
- Meditate on the goodness of God (Psalm 100:5)
- Praise **ELOHIM** and listen to songs of praise (Psalm 86:12)
- Meditate on The Word of God (Psalm 19:14)
- Show reverence to The Almighty Creator (1 Samuel 12:24)
- Follow Jesus' teachings and life examples (John 12:26)
- Fellowship with other followers of Jesus (Hebrews 10:25)
- Watch Bible teaching videos and/or read a Daily Devotional (Psalm 119:11)

The goal of this study was to give you a framework for how to engage in a comprehensive study of Scripture. As mentioned previously, a study can consist of: a specific book in the Bible; the life and teachings of a person, e.g., **YAHUSHUA**, Moses, or David; or exploring a particular theme, such as the application of wisdom, how to have patience, the importance of helping those in need, or what it means to love God.

Following are some verses to encourage and challenge you in your journey of growing in your relationship with The Great I AM.

Mark 12:30-31 (NIV)
30 Love the Lord your God with all your heart and with all your soul and with all your mind and with all your strength. 31 The second is this: Love your neighbor as yourself. There is no commandment greater than these."

1 Samuel 16:7 (NIV)
7 But the LORD said to Samuel, "Do not consider his appearance or his height, for I have rejected him. The LORD does not look at the things people look at. People look at the outward appearance, but the LORD looks at the heart."

Psalm 51:10 (NLT)
Create in me a clean heart, O God. Renew a loyal spirit within me.

Jeremiah 17:9-10 (NLT)
⁹ "The human heart is the most deceitful of all things, and desperately wicked. Who really knows how bad it is? ¹⁰ But I, the LORD, search all hearts and examine secret motives. I give all people their due rewards, according to what their actions deserve."

Hebrews 10:23-25 (NLT)
²³ Let us hold tightly without wavering to the hope we affirm, for God can be trusted to keep His promise. ²⁴ Let us think of ways to motivate one another to acts of love and good works. ²⁵ And let us not neglect our meeting together, as some people do, but encourage one another, especially now that the day of His return is drawing near.

2 Timothy 2:15 (KJV)
Study to shew thyself approved unto God, a workman that needeth not to be ashamed, rightly dividing the word of truth.

John 15:13 (NASB)
Greater love has no one than this, that a person will lay down his life for his friends.

1 John 4:9 (NCB)
God's love was revealed to us in this way: God sent His only-begotten Son into the world so that we might have life through Him.

John 3:16 (KJV)
For God so loved the world, that He gave His only begotten Son, that whosoever believeth in Him should not perish, but have everlasting life.

1 Corinthians 13:13 (NIV)
And now these three remain: faith, hope and love. But the greatest of these is love.

There are individuals that have extensive knowledge of the Bible, and yet their heart can be far from **YAHWEH**, and the teachings of Jesus. A person's title, position, credentials, influence, or affluence has absolutely nothing to do with character or a love for God. In the passage below, the Apostle Paul speaks about various motivations behind preaching Christ.

Philippians 1:18 (NIV)
But what does it matter? The important thing is that in every way, whether from false motives or true, Christ is preached. And because of this I rejoice. Yes, and I will continue to rejoice.

Paul's message is clear: regardless of the intentions—be they pure or impure, or self-serving—he finds joy in knowing that Christ is preached. It's through engaging with Scripture yourself that you'll discover the invaluable teachings, and learn how to live according to God's will.

Questions for Discussion:

1. What would you like to study in Scripture and why?

2. Why do you think it's important to get together with other believers?

3. Do you think there is one way, or many ways to grow in your faith? Explain.

4. How has this study changed the way you think about studying the Bible?

5. What are some things that stood out to you in this study?

6. What version of the Bible do you use? Will you use other versions? If so, why or why not?

7. How do you feel about learning the Hebrew names of God?

8. How will you incorporate time to study The Word of God?

Reflection:

Around my early 20's, I began reading the Bible on a regular basis when my father encouraged me to "stay in the Scriptures." I was reading all kinds of books and would have conversations with my father about what I had read. However, he cautioned me about authors and encouraged me to study the Bible. I'll never forget what my father said to me: *"La Wonda, books are good, but you read and study Scripture for yourself."* He never wanted me to rely on what anyone said even if it was a pastor or other church leader. As I started to make reading the Bible a daily practice, I didn't initially start by taking notes, however, I would reflect on the passages I read. Eventually, I read the Bible in its entirety and continued this practice. Over time, my reading evolved into a more structured study that included taking extensive notes, researching, and comparing various translations and transliterations of Scripture. This has helped me grow spiritually and has given me a deeper love for God.

Before I begin studying the Bible, I make it a practice to pray for understanding and wisdom from The Holy Spirit. Should you encounter difficulties with understanding a topic, verse, or passage, I recommend prayer and even a day or more of meditation on the material. If you are still unclear, then consider consulting Bible commentaries, dictionaries, or other resources for additional insight. Let this be a supplementary aid, ensuring that The Holy Spirit's guidance is your primary influence.

No matter where you find yourself in life, dedicate time to The Word of God—even if it's a short daily devotional. As a follower of Jesus, The Holy Spirit dwells within you. Pray and trust that through His presence, you will uncover truth, hope, guidance, peace, healing for both your body and mind, and an ever-growing love for The Almighty Creator.

My consistent prayer is that **YAHWEH** would give me a heart for Him and that I would love Him with all my heart, soul, might, and strength. This one prayer request, which is the first and greatest commandment, has given me a love for **ELOHIM** and His Word.

May your love for God, and your engagement with Scripture, enrich your spiritual journey profoundly.

Questions for Further Study:

- How do prayer, praise, worship, study, and fellowship work together?
- What does our Creator tell us about studying Scripture?
- Why is Mark 12:30 the greatest commandment?
- What insights have you learned from these lessons?

Your Reflections:

Additional responses to questions and/or notes:

I have shared stories about my father, Joseph Jerome Harris (11/26/1926 – 12/14/2005), who greatly influenced me. He was kind, compassionate, and strong, with a deep love for in-depth Bible study. A reserved man who loved the Lord, he was an example to his wife, six children, extended family, and friends.

The following is a tract my father wrote in the 1990s to hand out—not just to people he knew, but primarily to strangers. He was deeply concerned about everyone's soul. The content and cover design have been preserved exactly as he created them, without any modifications.

You may be someone who has money and power. You may also have a fine car, a new home, a good education, and a good job. It's also a good feeling when your doctor tells you that you are in perfect health. You may be one who gets along well with people and have many friends. Now you may say, "I have all this, so I don't need anything else." You may be one of those who say, "I don't have any of those things you just named, but if I did, I wouldn't have anything to worry about." Let's see if that's true.

Jesus told of a man in the Gospel of Luke, the 12th chapter starting with verse 16. "And he spake a parable unto them, saying, The ground of a certain rich man brought forth plentifully: And he thought within himself saying, What shall I do, because I have no room where to bestow my fruits? And he said, This will I do: I will pull down my barns, and build greater; and there will I bestow all my fruits and my goods. And I will say to my soul, Soul, thou hast much goods laid up for many years; take thine ease, eat, drink, and be merry. But God said unto him _Thou_ foul, this night thy soul shall be required of thee: then whose shall those things be, which thou has provided?" (Read Luke 12:16-20)

Now, let's look at this rich man for a moment. Look at what the man said concerning his soul, "Soul, thou hast much goods laid up for many years." Did he have many years? See what God said to him; "_Thou_ foul, this night thy soul shall be required of thee." The man died that night. James 4:14 says, "Whereas ye know not what _shall_ be on the morrow. For what _is_ your life? It is even a vapour, that appeareth for a little time, and then vanished away." Your life can be here today and gone tomorrow. In the gospel of Matthew 16:26, Jesus said, "what is a man profited, if he shall gain the whole world, and lose his own soul?" Back in the account of Luke 12, God didn't say anything was wrong with being rich, the problem was that the rich man did not make the right plans for his soul.

Now here's the Big Question . . .
ARE YOU SAVED?

Have you made any plans for your soul? It's not too late, don't wait for tomorrow, because today may be your tomorrow. You may ask, "what must I do?" Jesus did it all, he paid the price for your sins and mine. You need to realize you are a sinner and need to be saved. Romans 3:23 says, "all have sinned, and come short of the glory of God." The all includes you and me. You need to believe that Jesus died, was buried, and that he rose again the third day according to the scriptures in 1 Corinthians 15:3-4; read it for yourself.

Romans 10:9-10 says, "that (put your name here) if thou shalt confess with thy mouth the Lord Jesus, and shalt believe in thine heart that God hath raised him from the dead, thou shalt be saved. For with the heart man believeth unto righteousness; and with the mouth confession is made unto salvation." Romans 10:13 says, "For whosoever (that's you) shall call upon the name of the Lord shall be saved." It doesn't say, "may be saved" or "I think so", the Bible says, if you call, God will save you. How do I know this, because over thirty years ago I called on God to save me and he did just that. If you are in Maryland and need directions to Florida, I can give them to you because I've been there. The reason why I wrote this booklet is because ever since God saved me, I have a burden for lost souls. The Bible says in II Peter 3:9, It's not God's will "that any should perish, but that all should come to repentance."

St. John 3:16 says, "For God so loved the world, that he gave his only begotten Son, that whosoever (that's you) believeth in him should not perish, but have everlasting life." Friend would you bow your head right now and in your own words pray, and ask God to save you. He will. The Bible says in Titus 1:2 that God cannot lie. Your next step is to read God's word each day so you can grow in the Christian life. A good place to start is to read and study the gospel of John and the book of Romans.

Don't wait, to make plans for your soul, do it now, tomorrow may be too late!

J. Harris

www.ingramcontent.com/pod-product-compliance
Lightning Source LLC
Chambersburg PA
CBHW041121120626
46547CB00019B/2809